Jon Marks and Alison Wooder

The London game
A challenge for Dave

Ernst Klett Verlag
Stuttgart · Leipzig

Contents

Before you read the story

1 Your digital life

*Imagine that you're going to London tomorrow and you can bring
only **one** of these things. Which are you going to bring? Explain why.*

- A basic mobile phone (you can call and send text messages,
  but you can't use the internet).
- A laptop computer with wi-fi.
- A smartphone with a problem – you can send messages and see
  websites, but you can't call someone.

2 What do you know about London?

Do you know / Can you guess the answers to these questions?

1. Greenwich is …
   a) by the river Thames.
   b) a town near London.
   c) the oldest part of London.

2. The National Maritime Museum
   is …
   a) full of old cars.
   b) full of modern art.
   c) full of old ships.

3. Cutty Sark is an old ship that …
   a) is now a museum.
   b) is in a museum.
   c) still travels on the Thames.

4. London buses are …
   a) blue.
   b) red.
   c) green.

5. The Underground or 'Tube' is a
   kind of public … in London.
   a) theatre
   b) school
   c) transport

6. At Buckingham Palace tourists
   like to see …
   a) the Changing of the Guard.
   b) the crown jewels.
   c) a famous painting of William
      Shakespeare.

7. A Beefeater …
   a) is a policeman.
   b) works in the Tower of London.
   c) eats only burgers.

8. An Oyster card is …
   a) a travel card.
   b) a birthday card with an oyster.
   c) seafood.

1 Computer games are (not) boring

Ping!

It was Saturday morning, and Dave was in his bedroom. The sound came from under a pile of computer game magazines. It was a new message on his phone. He moved the magazines, and picked up his phone. The message was from Luke: *I'm in Casa Coffee with Jay. It's that* 5 *new café in Greenwich. Want to join us?*

Dave typed a reply.

Y R U in a café?

Ping! It was a reply from Luke.

Have you forgotten how to write words?! 10

Dave laughed and sent another reply.

OK, I'll try again! Why are you in a café?

Ping!

It's raining. Jay's house is full of uncles, aunts and cousins, and in mine there's a guy fixing the washing machine. A pipe broke and there's water 15 *all over the kitchen floor!*

Dave tapped his reply: *OK.*

Ping!

Do U know where it is?

Dave tapped on his phone again. 20

No, but I can find it with the map app on my phone.

Ping!

Can you tell Olivia, Holly and Gwen?

OK.

Dave thought for a moment. He sent Olivia an instant message so he 25 could see right away when she read it. Holly didn't have a computer or a smartphone, so he sent her an SMS text message. For Gwen, it was more practical to call her on her mobile. It was difficult for her to read messages.

Five minutes later, Dave sent another message to Luke. 30

& OK 4 O, H & G. C U 10 a.m.

Ping!

WHAT????? Luke replied to Dave.

Ha ha! Also OK for Olivia, Holly and Gwen. See you at 10 o'clock.

• • •

When Dave arrived at the café, all the others were already there. Jay and Luke had glasses of lemonade. In front of them were two plates – empty plates.

"The cakes here are amazing!" said Jay. "I had chocolate and Luke had
5 lemon. I ate some of his, and he ate some of mine. They were the best cakes we've ever had!"

"And of course you didn't save any for us!" said Holly.

"Oh, sorry," said Jay, "the cakes were just *too* good to save. And we bought them with *our* pocket money! Why don't you buy some for
10 yourselves?"

"Good idea!" said Dave.

"Problem," said Gwen.

"How much money have you got, Dave?" asked Olivia.

Dave took some coins from his pocket.
15 "About £1.50," he said.

"We've only got £3.50," said Olivia. "With your £1.50, that's £5. It's not enough for four cakes. It's not even enough for four glasses of lemonade! Can we borrow some money from you?"

"Sorry," said Luke, "we can't help you. We've spent all our money."

"Yeah, on delicious cakes for you to eat alone," said Holly. 5 She pretended to be Luke with a piece of cake in his hand. "Mmmm! I'm *so* enjoying this *delicious* cake. Jay, should we save some for our dear friends Holly, Olivia, Gwen and Dave?"

Then Olivia pretended to be Jay with a piece of cake in his hand. "No Luke. I don't want to share any with them. Let's eat it *all!*" 10

"You're overreacting. It was just two pieces of cake. And I don't talk like that!" said Jay.

"Yes, you do! Ha ha!" said Luke. Jay pushed him, and some of Luke's lemonade went on the table.

"Hey hey, calm down!" Dave said to the two of them as he tried to 15 mediate their little fight. He turned to the girls. "I know what to do. We can ask for three glasses of lemonade, and an extra glass. Maybe we could try the cakes next time we're here."

. . .

"Wow! Have you just won a lot of money?" said the waitress a few minutes later after she wrote down what they wanted. 20

"No," said Dave. "We're spending our pocket money."

"Dave, she's joking!" whispered Gwen.

"Now we're really not going to get *Skateboarding Wizards II*," said Luke to Dave. "Not with our pocket money."

"True," said Dave. 25

"What's *Skateboarding Wizards II*?" asked Holly.

"It's a computer game," said Dave. "The first one is fantastic. There are some wizards, and they've all got skateboards, and they're in a big scary castle, and they have to find a ..."

"It sounds very boring!" said Olivia. 30

"It's not boring," replied Luke. "I've played it for hours with Dave. It's really exciting."

"And my computer game magazine says the new one is even better," said Dave. "More wizards, faster skateboards, a bigger castle ..."

"Anyway, you can't have it," said Holly. "You haven't got the money to buy it."

"It's your birthday soon," said Jay. "Ask your parents for the game."

"They don't give me computer games. They say that I spend too much time on my computer," said Dave. "They don't understand that I'm not wasting time. I'm learning about computers."

"And skateboarding wizards," said Olivia.

"Adults have no understanding of how we teens use technology," said Holly. "My mum says I don't need a smartphone. She thinks this old phone from about a million years ago is good enough for me."

She showed her small, grey, very old mobile.

"My grandparents haven't even got a mobile phone," said Luke. "The only media they care about are newspapers, radio and TV! They haven't got a computer or a tablet or even an e-mail address. Imagine that! I wanted to e-mail them a photo of me and my football team, but I couldn't! I had to send it to them in a letter so they could have a print copy!"

"Old people have no idea about technology!" said Dave.

"Excuse *me!*" came a voice from behind them. "I cannot *believe* what you kids are saying!"

"Oh … er … hello, Granny Rose, I didn't see you here when I came in," said Dave and tried not to sound embarrassed. "This is my grandmother," he said to his friends.

"You think I have no idea about technology?" said Granny Rose. "You see those people over there?" She pointed to a group of people at another table. They were all older than 60, and each one had a laptop or a tablet. "That's my club. We all love technology. We meet once a week to help each other with our computers and smartphones and to learn new things about them. We even read computer magazines for the tips. We're the Silver Surfers."

"Er … do you surf in the sea, too?" said Dave, trying to make a joke.

"Very funny. We surf the internet and we all have silver hair, so we're the Silver Surfers."

Then Dave had an idea. "Do you like computer games?" he asked.

"I don't. A couple of the others do, but they're not computer game mad," said Granny Rose. "Our main interest is using technology for communication. You know, to stay in touch with family and friends."

"I *love* computer games," said Dave. "My favourite is *Skateboarding Wizards*. Did you know that there's *Skateboarding Wizards II* now?"

"And it's your birthday soon. Yes, I heard. I also know your parents' opinion about computer games. I'm going back to my friends now. Bye."

"That was clever, Dave," said Jay when Granny Rose was with her friends again. "Now your grandmother knows you want that game."

"Do you think she'll give it to you for your birthday?" asked Gwen.

"I don't know," said Dave. "She may, she may not. Sometimes I just don't understand her. She can be very mysterious."

2 A strange message

It was the evening of the same day. Luke and Dave were at Dave's house, on the floor in the living room. On the TV in front of them was Dave's newest computer game.

"Ha! I hit you!" said Dave. He had headphones on his head. This made
5 him speak in a loud voice.

On the TV, a wizard fell off a skateboard.

"Ohhhhhh!" cried Luke. He had headphones on his head too.

"I win, you lose! I win, you lose!" Dave shouted. "I'm always the winner!"

10 "A winner with a very big head! You say that whenever you win, but you don't *always* win," said Luke. He took off his headphones, and Dave did the same. "Anyway, you play it more than I do so you don't need to show off. Do you want to play again?"

They heard the front door of Dave's house open. Then there was a
15 click as the living room door knob turned, and Dave's mother came into the room. "Hello, boys," she said. "I need the TV now. *Let's Cook!* is on in five minutes."

"Erghh!" said Dave. "Boring!"

"Well, it's my favourite programme of the week. Now go on up to your bedroom," said Dave's mum. "And take this mess with you when you go." She pointed to their bags, jackets and other things on the floor.

The boys carried their things upstairs. When they were in Dave's 5 bedroom, he turned on his laptop.

"Can we play *Skateboarding Wizards* on your computer?" asked Luke.

"No," said Dave. "We can only play that downstairs."

"Should we just watch a video?" Luke asked.

"No, we can play a different game on my laptop. Oh ... I've got a new 10 message ... That's strange."

"What's strange?" Luke wanted to know.

"This message," said Dave. "Come and read it."

Luke looked at the laptop screen.

```
A CHALLENGE FROM THE SILVER SURFERS
Find the answers to our puzzles, exactly three,
And get the game you want from my friends and me.
If you can't do this, then no internet for you.
A week without, no computer games and no smartphone too.
```

"It's not a very good poem," said Luke. 15

"It's an awful poem! But what does it mean?" asked Dave.

"I think it's some kind of game from your grandmother and her Silver Surfer friends," said Luke. "You have to find the answers to three puzzles. If you can, you get *Skateboarding Wizards II*. If you can't, you have to spend a week without the internet, without computer games 20 and without your mobile phone."

Another message came onto the screen.

```
Find the correct answers, or you must follow that rule!
Start tomorrow, it's going to be cool!
Your friends can help you, up to three.
This is the challenge. Do you agree?
```

"The second part of the poem is even worse!" said Luke.

"Since when does Granny say 'cool'? Hmm. It says I can ask three friends to help me," said Dave.

"Who are you going to ask?" Luke wanted to know.

5 "Well, not you," replied Dave.

"Oh," said Luke in a sad voice.

"I'm joking!" laughed Dave. "Of course I want you to take part in the challenge. But which of the others are we going to ask?"

"That's easy," said Luke. "Tomorrow Gwen is going to go camping
10 with her family, and Jay is going to visit his grandparents. He goes every Sunday afternoon, never misses it. So it's Holly and Olivia."

"Great! But we need to ask them first. I'll call Holly. You can text Olivia, OK?"

• • •

Five minutes later, Dave put his phone in his pocket.

15 "That was a long discussion with Holly," said Dave. "It was difficult to persuade her. It's her mum's birthday tomorrow."

"Yes, I heard," said Luke. "But she's going to come?"

"Yes, she is," said Dave. "What about Olivia?"

"I don't know," said Luke. "She hasn't replied yet. Oh, here's her reply
20 now." He picked up his phone and looked at it.

"What does she say?" asked Dave.

"She says, 'OK, but if this is a silly joke, you're in BIG trouble!' Well, I hope it *isn't* a silly joke."

Dave sat down in front of his computer. He took a deep breath and
25 under the poem, he typed "I agree." A few moments later, a reply came.

```
Be in the centre of Greenwich tomorrow at 2 p.m.
Bring your phone.
```

3 I have sails but no wind can reach me

It was 2 p.m. the next day – Sunday. Dave, Luke, Holly and Olivia met at their favourite bench in Greenwich Park.

"Is this some kind of game?" asked Holly.

"Yeah, that's right," said Dave. "Granny Rose loves games and puzzles."

"I like your granny," said Olivia. "She's fun."   5

"I think the other Silver Surfers are behind this too," said Luke.

Ping!

Dave took his phone out of his pocket, and opened his messages.

"Aha! It's her! Or them – the Silver Surfers. The game is on!"

"What does it say?" asked Holly.   10

"Er ... I don't really understand it," said Dave, "but I'll read what it says: 'I have sails but no wind can reach me.'"

"What on earth does that mean?" asked Luke.

"Old ships have sails," said Olivia. "You know, the wind pushes the ship."

"Wait! Now I understand! It's a riddle," said Holly. "You know, a puzzle where someone gives you clues and you must find the answer. Here's one: 'What word becomes shorter when you add two letters?'"

"That's an old one," said Dave.

"Old one?" said Luke. "I haven't heard it."

"Short!" said Dave.

"I don't get it," said Luke.

"Short plus E and R makes 'shorter'."

"Oh yeah," said Luke.

"But I don't get this one from the Silver Surfers," said Olivia. "'I have sails ...' OK, that's clear. It means an old ship. '... but no wind can reach me.' I don't understand that part."

Ping!

"Another message," said Dave. "It says 'Send a photo as soon as you find it. You have one hour.'" He thought for a moment. "Maybe it's Cutty Sark. Remember when we went there last year, Luke?"

"Of course," said Luke. "We met an old sailor, and he told us a story about the ship. OK, Cutty Sark has sails, but wind *can* reach it. It's outside, next to the river. 'No wind can reach me', remember? That means somewhere indoors."

"A ship indoors? Maybe we need some help here," said Dave. "I'm going to look for an answer online."

"What about the rules of the challenge?" asked Holly. "Is it fair if you use the internet for help?"

"Why not?" said Dave. "The Silver Surfers didn't say anything about that. OK, I'm going to search for 'Greenwich ships indoors'. Oops! I typed Greebwich!"

"Hurry up, Dave!" said Luke. "We're taking too much time! We've only got an hour, remember? And we've already used nearly five minutes."

"Here we are," said Dave. "Oh yes, of course! The National Maritime Museum. That's a good place to look for boats and ships inside a building. Let's go! It's next to the park, about a five minute walk from here."

The four friends walked across the park until they reached the National Maritime Museum. They went around the building until they came to the entrance.

"What about tickets?" asked Holly. "I haven't got any money."

"Don't worry," said Olivia. "It's free. Haven't you been here before?"

"No, never," said Holly. "I knew it was here, but I always thought, 'I needn't go there now. I can visit it any time I want.'"

"I was there only once, when I was about six," said Dave. 5

"It's a great museum!" said Olivia. "OK, we haven't got time now, but you should come and visit it."

"Well, thanks for the advice," said Dave, "but now we must find this ship!"

• • •

Half an hour later the friends were back in the entrance hall. 10

"We've been in every room in the museum," said Luke. "We've seen pictures of ships, parts of ships, models of ships. Maybe one of those is the ship in the riddle."

"But which one? We still don't have an answer!" Olivia replied. "Hmm. Let me think." She made some notes on a piece of paper. A strong wind 15 came through an open window and almost blew them away.

"Maybe someone should close that window," Holly said.

"Those windows mean that wind can reach all of these ships," said Olivia. "Maybe this museum *isn't* the right place."

"Wait! Look!" said Holly. She tapped Olivia on the shoulder and 20 pointed outside.

"Of course!" said Olivia.

"What's going on? Have they gone crazy?" Luke asked Dave, as Olivia and Holly ran towards the door. The boys followed.

"Hey, slow down!" said a guard near the door. 25

"Sorry!" shouted Holly, but they all ran faster.

Outside the entrance, they stopped next to the museum's famous work of art. It was a big model of an old ship inside a very big bottle. There was a sign under it.

"It's called '*Nelson's Ship in a Bottle*,'" said Luke. "Who's Nelson?" 30

"Who *was* Nelson," said Olivia. "Were you asleep in History last term? He was Britain's most famous sailor. He won a big battle against the French in eighteen something."

"The Battle of Trafalgar, 1805. He won the battle, but he died on his ship," said Dave.

"Very good!" said Olivia. "Did you remember that from the lesson?"

"No, I just looked it up on the internet," said Dave.

5   "Well, no wind can reach *that* ship!" said Dave. "I think we've found the answer. Now we need to send a photo to the Silver Surfers."

"There's no hurry. We've still got ten minutes," said Holly. "Let's get a nice group photo! Excuse me!"

There was a man with grey hair on a bench near the ship in a bottle.

10   "Can you take a photo of us, please?"

"OK, sure," said the man.

"Whose phone has the best camera?" asked Holly.

"Mine has got a very good camera," said Dave, and gave his phone to the man. "To take a photo, you have to press this …"

15   "I know, I know," said the man. "Ready? Smile!"

He took the photo, and gave the phone back to Dave. Dave looked at the result.

"Nice photo, thanks!" he said to the man. Then he turned to the others. "I'm going to send it to the Silver Surfers."

The man started to walk away. He turned and smiled at them, then 5 walked round the corner of the museum.

"That man," said Holly. "I think I've seen him before. I know! He was in the café, yesterday. He's one of the Silver Surfers."

"Look," said Olivia. "He's left an envelope on the bench. It says 'Dave' on it." 10

Dave went to the bench and picked it up.

"Well, open it!" said Luke.

Dave took out four small cards.

"They're day tickets," he said. "You know, for the Tube and buses. You can have any number of journeys in one day. And there's a map of 15 all the London Tube lines."

Ping!

Dave looked at his phone. "It's a reply from the Silver Surfers," he said. "With the next challenge."

4 Tube map puzzle

"So what *is* the next challenge?" asked Luke. "Come on, we're waiting!"

"It's another strange one," said Dave. It just says 'Take the Tube,' and then there are two emojis."

"Let me see," said Luke and took Dave's phone.

TAKE THE TUBE

5   "That *is* strange," he said, and passed the phone to Olivia. Holly looked over Olivia's shoulder at the phone.

"What's this about?" asked Luke. "'Take the Tube' that means take the Underground. That's clear. But why have they sent us the elephant emoji and the castle emoji?"

10   "Just link the two ideas," said Holly. "It means the Elephant and Castle Tube station. Look at the Tube map."

Dave took the Tube map out of the envelope, and opened it. "Yes, of course you're right," he said. "We must go there."

Ping! It was another message from the Silver Surfers.

15   *Have you worked it out yet?*

Yes, replied Dave.

Ping!

Good! Send a selfie when you get there.

"So what's the best way to get to Elephant and Castle?" asked Dave.

20   "Let's have a look at the Tube map again," said Holly. Her family didn't have a car, and they often used the Tube. "Hmm. We should go over to Cutty Sark station, and go north on the DLR. Then we should change to the Jubilee line and go west. At London Bridge, we should change to the Northern line, and then it's just two stops down to Elephant and Castle."

25   "That way we'll have to change trains *twice*," said Luke. "Isn't there a simpler way to do it?"

"You look at the map, then, Mr I'm-So-Clever," said Holly. "Can you see a better way?"

Luke looked at the map. "Oh, sorry, Holly," he said after a while. "You're right. Your way is the best way."

• • •

Half an hour later, the friends were on the platform of Elephant and Castle Tube station. They stood in front of the station sign, and Dave took a selfie. Then he tried to send it.

"Oh yes, of course," he said. "I can't send it from here. We're under the ground. My phone doesn't work because there's no mobile phone signal down here! We'll have to go up to the street."

They went up from the platform and out of the station. The streets were very busy, and there were lots of big, modern buildings.

"OK, I'm sending that selfie now," said Dave.

A few seconds later, a reply came: It was the 'thumbs up' emoji.

"Our answer was right!" said Dave.

Another message came. This time it was two emojis:

The friends all looked at Dave's phone together.

"What does that mean?" asked Luke.

"The first one's easy," said Dave. "It's the flag of the European Union.

So that could mean Europe, or just the letters EU. But I don't know the second one. I've never seen it before."

"What is it? Some kind of statue?" asked Luke.

"Yeah, I think it is," said Dave. "I can find out what it means online. 5 Just give me a moment … Aha! OK, it can mean statue, stone, hard or head. But what does that mean? Europe statue, EU statue, Europe stone, EU stone …"

"Euston!" said Holly. "E plus U plus stone … Euston. It's another Tube station."

10 "You're good at this, Holly!" said Olivia. "What's the best way to get there?"

Dave gave Holly the map.

"That's easy," she said. "It's nine stops north of here. We have to go two stops up to Waterloo, then change lines."

15 "Let's go!" said Dave.

• • •

Twenty minutes later the friends were outside Euston Tube station. Dave sent another selfie of all of them in front of the station sign. Soon after, the reply came: another 'thumbs up' emoji. Then a second message came, with two more emojis.

20 "*Another* Tube trip!" said Luke. "Why? What do the Silver Surfers want?"

"I'm sure we'll find out soon," said Olivia. "Which station is it this time?"

"What do you think, Holly?" asked Dave and passed her the phone. 25 "You're the expert on Tube stations."

"Hmm. I know that emoji. It means 'city'. And the other one is a bridge. City plus bridge."

"Any ideas?" asked Olivia.

"Er, let me think ... London Bridge!" said Holly. "The city is *this* city – London. Remember how we changed trains at London Bridge before we arrived at Elephant and Castle."

"Well done, Holly!" said Luke. "That's amazing!"   5

"We don't need to change this time," said Holly. "The line goes east for two stops, then turns south, and goes down to London Bridge."

"Let's go!" said Olivia.

• • •

Outside London Bridge Tube station, Dave sent another selfie to the Silver Surfers. After a few moments, the reply came. It was another   10 'thumbs up', two more emojis and two words:

LAST STATION!

"Holly?" said Dave and passed her the phone.

"Waterloo," said Holly. "We changed lines there on the way to Euston."

"Wow!" said Dave. "That was quick. But how did you work that out? I don't get it."   15

"This one means water," said Holly, and pointed at the first emoji. "How many Tube stations begin with 'Water'?"

"Good point. But why is there the toilet emoji?"

"'Loo' of course. Don't you sometimes call the toilet the loo?"

"Oh, yeah, of course. Now I get it!" said Dave. "Water plus loo –   20 Waterloo. Let's go to Waterloo station – again. It's just two stops west from here, right?"

"You're learning," said Holly.

• • •

"So, last station," said Dave. "Now I hope we'll find out why we're here."

The friends were outside Waterloo, one of the biggest, busiest stations in London.

5 **Ping!** It was another message on Dave's phone. "What does it say?" asked Luke.

"'Now find the letter.'" said Dave. "That's all."

"Find a letter? What letter?" asked Luke. "I can't see any letters. Can *you*? How can we find a letter in this station? It's huge!"

10 "No, *the* letter, not *a* letter," said Dave.

"Maybe it's a letter of the alphabet, not a letter in an envelope," said Olivia. "But which letter? Look at all of these signs on the walls. Almost every letter of the alphabet is there."

"I may have an idea," said Holly. "Who's got the Tube map?"

15 "Here," said Luke and passed it to her. She opened it.

"Look," she said. "The first station was Elephant and Castle."

"The first station was Cutty Sark," said Olivia.

"Yeah, but the first station *in emojis* was Elephant and Castle. From there we went north to Euston, then east for a bit, and then we turned 20 south to London Bridge. After that we went west, back to Waterloo. Watch me follow our journey on the map." She moved her finger from each station to the next. "Our journey made the shape of the letter 'P'.*"

"Holly, you're a genius!" said Dave.

"I'm not a genius. I just use the Tube a lot," said Holly. "I'm not usually very good at maps and stuff."

"You're always too self-critical," said Dave, and then, "Oh sorry!"

"Why did you say 'sorry'?" asked Olivia. 5

"That woman there bumped into me," Dave pointed to a woman with grey hair. Now she was a few metres away.

"Wait a minute," said Luke. "That woman ... I've seen her before too. She's another of the Silver Surfers!"

"Have you sent that message to them yet, Dave?" asked Olivia. 10

"No, I haven't. What should I send? Just the letter P?" said Dave.

"Yeah," said Olivia. "Go on, try it."

Dave tapped just 'P', then sent the message. Soon after, the reply came: another 'thumbs up' emoji.

"Well, we're finished with that puzzle!" said Dave. "Let's see what 15 happens next."

A minute later, another message came: *Look in your pocket!*

Dave felt in his jacket pocket and found an envelope.

* To find a map, go to the 'Transport of London' website.

5 The oldest thing in the City of London

Dave opened the envelope. Inside, there were two pieces of paper. He opened one. There was a message on it. He showed it to his friends.

Dear Dave,

What's the oldest thing in the City of London?
Your answer must ARRIVE in one hour.

Yours,
The Silver Surfers.

"How can we answer that?" said Luke. "London's a *huge* city!"

Holly pointed at the envelope. "What's that other piece of paper?" she
5 asked. Dave took it out of the envelope.

"It's a map of the old centre of London," he said. "Just the part between St Paul's Cathedral and the Tower of London."

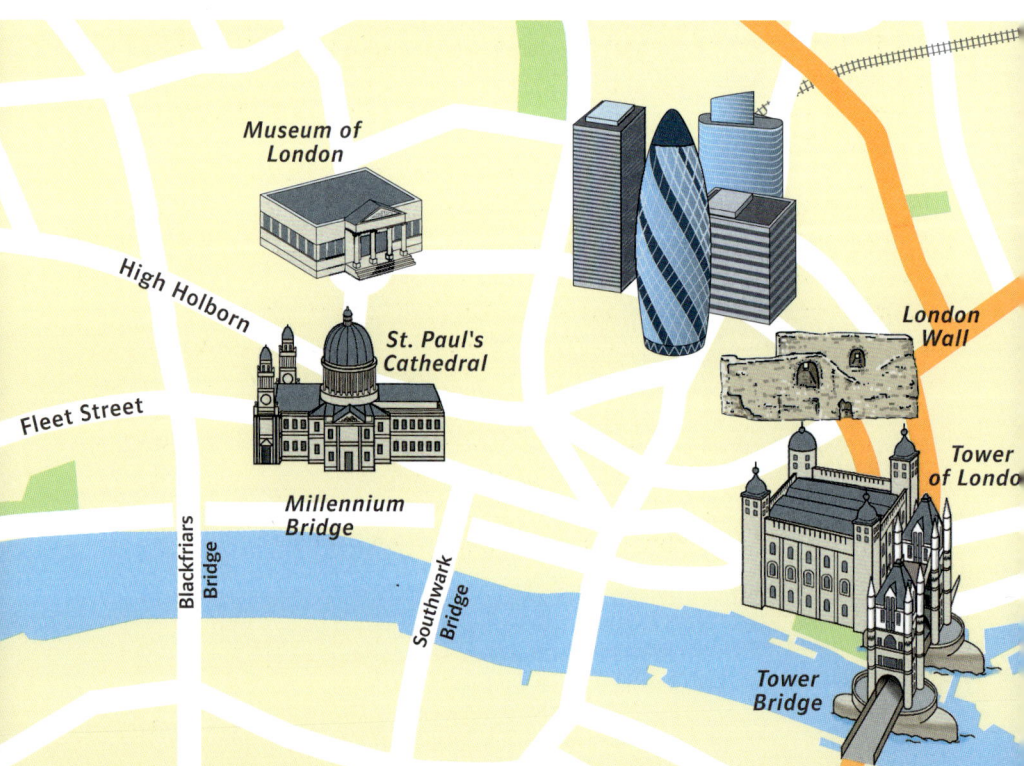

"That's the City of London in the question. 'City of London' is the name for the oldest part of the centre of London."

"You're right," said Dave. "OK. Let's think. Where can we look for the oldest thing in the City of London?"

"The British Museum?" asked Olivia. 5

"I don't think so," said Luke. He took the City of London map from Dave. "No. You see, the British Museum isn't in the City of London. The only museum I can see on this map is the Museum of London. Should we try there? What do you think?"

"I can't think of a better place to look," said Dave. "What's the time 10 now?"

"It's five o'clock," said Luke.

"We need to check the opening times. I can find out on the internet."

He took his phone out of his pocket. He typed 'Museum of London' into the search window, then pressed 'Go'. 15

"Nothing's happening," said Luke. "Maybe your phone has crashed."

"Give it a chance," said Dave. "Mobile internet is often slow. Aha! Here are the opening times … It's open until six o'clock. Great, no problem! Let's go! Oh … how are we going to get there?"

Holly took the City of London map from Luke. "We shouldn't try to get 20 to the Museum of London by Tube because it isn't near a Tube station," she said. "I think we need to get a bus. We can use these day tickets on the buses too, remember?"

There were lots of different bus stops around them outside Waterloo station, and hundreds of people. 25

"Which bus stop do we need?" asked Dave. "Let's ask somebody."

"Who?" said Luke. "All these people are travelling too, to lots of different places. I don't think anybody will be able to tell us."

"Maybe there's a bus map on the wall," said Olivia.

"Maybe, but I can't see it," said Dave. "But it's easy! I can just find out 30 online again. I've done this a million times before." He typed 'Waterloo to Museum of London bus number' into the search window.

"Aha! Here we are!" he said. "I've found a travellers' advice forum. OK … somebody asked the same question, and another member of the forum posted an answer. We need a number 59." 35

"There's a 59 coming now!" shouted Luke.

The friends ran to the bus stop and jumped onto the bus.

"Let's go upstairs," said Holly. "It's much more fun upstairs on a bus."

They went up. Holly and Dave sat down in the front seats, and Olivia and Luke sat behind them.

"These are the best seats on the bus!" said Holly.

5 The bus went over the river, and turned right. In the distance they could see the round top of St Paul's Cathedral. Then the bus turned left and went north. After a few minutes, Holly held the map in the light from the bus window, and looked at it. "I don't think this is right," she said.

10 "What's the problem, Holly?" asked Olivia.

"We should be near the museum now, but we're not." Holly pointed at a place near the top of the map. "We shouldn't be in this street. Now we're going *away* from the museum."

"What's that building there?" asked Dave, and pointed out of the window.

"That's the British Museum," said Holly. "That's not the museum we want. It isn't inside the old City of London, remember?"

"May I see your phone, Dave?" said Olivia. She took his phone and looked at the travellers' advice forum. "Oh, Dave! You didn't read under the first reply to the post. Someone commented on it! It says 'The reply above is WRONG! A 59 is good for the British Museum, but for the Museum of London, you need a 100.' Dave, we're on the wrong bus!"

"Oh, er ... sorry, guys. So what can we do now?" asked Dave.

"We can just change to another bus," said Holly. "Dave, can you download an app for London transport onto your phone?"

"Of course, no problem," said Dave, and looked for one. "Aha! Here's a nice app!" he said. "Wait a moment for it to download ... OK, it's there. Ooh! It knows where we are right now! Wow! So I just type in 'Museum of London', then click here and ... here's the information! Great – it's not a disaster. We can get off the bus at the next stop, and get on a number 38."

"Great," said Luke. "The bus is stopping now. Let's go downstairs."

• • •

Twenty minutes later, the friends were outside the Museum of London.

"What time is it?" asked Dave.

"Quarter to six," said Luke. "That means we've only got 15 minutes to find the answer!"

The friends ran into the museum.

"Hey, don't run!" said a woman in uniform near the door.

"Sorry!" shouted Holly, and they all ran faster. Then Olivia stopped, and the others stopped too.

"We can't just run round the whole museum for the next 15 minutes," she said. "We're wasting time! We need to stop and think."

"Look, here's a map of the museum," said Luke, and pointed to a map on the wall. "Which section of the museum has the oldest things? The Roman section?"

"No," said Olivia. "It's the prehistoric section. That was the time before the Romans were here – hundreds of years before the Romans."

A minute later they arrived in the prehistoric section. It was full of things from thousands of years ago – things people made and used in
5 their lives.

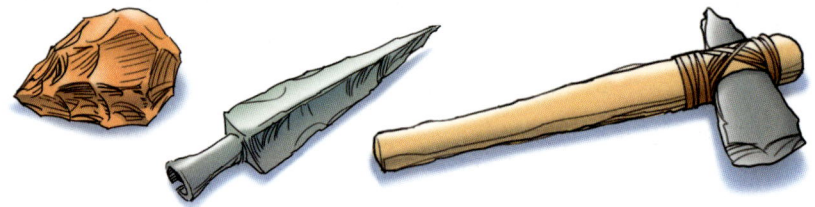

"But there are no exact dates here, so I don't know which one is the oldest," said Dave. "I don't know what to do! It's hopeless!"

"Now calm down, Dave!" said Olivia, "There's no such thing as a hopeless situation. Oh, I sound like an agony aunt!"

10 "We could say 'The things in the prehistoric section of the Museum of London?'" said Holly.

"I don't think that's right," said Olivia. "The question said 'thing', not 'things'."

"Well, have you got a better idea?" said Dave.

15 "Er … no," said Olivia.

Luke looked at his watch. "Hurry! You've got about two minutes to send the answer," he said.

"OK, let's try it anyway," said Dave. He sent a message to the Silver Surfers: *The things in the prehistoric section of the Museum of London.*

20 A minute later he received the reply:

```
A very good try, but it's not correct.
We're sorry you didn't get the clue.
Enjoy your week smartphone and computer free.
We're sure it will be good for you!
```

"Why are you laughing, Luke?" he said. "And now you too?" he said to Holly and Olivia. "What's so funny? This isn't making me feel better!"

"Your face!" said Luke. "You look like you're going to cry!"

6 No internet for a week!

The next day was Monday. There was no school because it was the half term holiday. The six friends met in Greenwich Park, at their favourite bench again. Luke, Holly and Gwen sat down on the bench. Dave, Olivia and Jay sat down on the grass, near some flowers. It was a beautiful sunny morning. There were not very many people in the park because 5 it was a weekday.

"What happened to that really bad weather forecast you saw on the internet, Jay?" asked Gwen. "'It's going to rain all day, with thunder and lightning ...' That's what you said."

"Wrong London," said Jay. "That was the forecast for London, *Canada*. 10 Sorry!"

"Never mind the weather!" said Dave. "What am I going to do? I mustn't use the internet for a week. No mobile phone, no computer games, nothing!"

"Well, the Silver Surfers aren't watching you," said Luke. "How are 15 they going to know? And what are they going to do about it anyway?"

"Maybe there could be a compromise," said Jay. "You got two answers right, so you could still use the internet a bit."

"No, no," said Dave. "A promise is a promise. I made a bet and I lost. Games have rules, and we must follow those rules." 20

"Exactly," said Olivia. "Of course you're going to keep your promise."

"But it *is* going to be awful," said Dave. "All this week you guys are going to send each other messages. How am I going to stay in touch? I'm going to feel left out. Maybe I should just stay away from you for the rest of the week." 25

"I've got a better idea," said Gwen. "Let's all join Dave. Let's *all* have no internet and phones for a week. We can do it for fun!"

"What? We're going to act like there are no mobile phones, no internet and no computer games?" said Luke. "What on earth are you talking about?" 30

"Oh, come on!" said Gwen. "It wouldn't be the end of the world! When my mum was a kid, they sometimes had power cuts so everything went black and they had to spend the evenings in candlelight. *We're* only talking about a week without smartphones, computer games or the internet." 35

"It could be fun," said Holly. "No nasty posts people put on social networks just to get attention, no comments on somebody's comment about somebody else's comment. No cyber bullies to block … I think it's a great idea."

5 "OK, you're right. I'm in," said Luke. "There's still TV, newspapers and the radio. We don't need to be bored."

"I agree!" said Jay. "Let's have a one-week holiday from the internet. I just need to tell all my friends what we've decided to do."

He took his phone out of his pocket.

10 "Er, Jay …" said Olivia.

"Oh, have we started already?" asked Jay.

"Yes," said Olivia. "We have."

"We should at least post a message for them, to say we're going offline," said Luke.

15 "Too late!" said Olivia, and took his phone from his hand.

"Anyway, what other friends?" asked Jay.

"Very funny," said Luke.

"I think somebody should look after our phones," said Holly. "That way, we *can't* use them. What about you?" she said to Gwen. "You don't
20 use yours very much anyway."

"OK, fine," said Gwen. "Put them in here," and she opened her bag.

"Goodbye!" said Dave to his phone in a sad voice, and put it in Gwen's bag.

"There's no need to be so upset," she said. "You're acting like you're
25 saying goodbye forever to your best friend!"

• • •

It was Wednesday morning, day three of the technology-free week. The friends were in Greenwich, next to the river.

"It wasn't easy to organise a time and place to meet!" said Luke. "How many phone calls was it? Ten?"

30 "It's lucky all our families have landlines," said Dave. "Without that, I don't know *how* we could meet. But, you know, I'm enjoying myself. It's different without smartphones and computers and stuff like that."

"We're spending more time together," said Holly. "Maybe because we have to chat face-to-face, not by texts and messages."

"So what are we going to do today?" asked Jay.

"How about a walk along the river?" said Olivia. "We could walk towards the centre of London. There are lots of interesting things to see."

"I've never done that," said Luke. "And I've lived in Greenwich all my life." 5

"Are you sure we *can* walk along the river all the way?" asked Dave. "We can't look at a map app to find out."

"Aha! I almost forgot!" said Holly. "I found my mum's old London map book. I always carry it with me now that I can't use internet maps."

She took it out of her bag. They looked at it and found that it was 10 possible to walk along the river all the way to the centre of London.

"Centre of London, here we come!" said Luke.

They went past Canary Wharf on the other side of the river, with its big, modern office buildings. Then they came to the old docks.

"How do we get out of here?" asked Jay. "We could go that way behind 15 the café or that way over the little bridge or that way between the two office blocks."

"Hmm. This area has changed since my mum bought the map book," said Holly. "I don't know where to go."

"We can ask somebody," said Olivia. "Excuse me!" She waved at a 20 young woman at a table outside the café. "What's the best way to get to the centre of London?"

"Er, that way," said the woman, and pointed to the little bridge. She had a book in her hands and when she pointed, she dropped it and it hit the ground with a bang. Olivia picked it up. "Victorian London," she 25 said, reading the title. "Interesting book?"

"It's very interesting," said the woman. "In Queen Victoria's time, ships arrived right here from all parts of the world. These old buildings were full of amazing things from other countries. Now they're all flats, offices, cafés and shops." 30

The others came over to the table, and they had a conversation with the woman. She was a History student from Spain. She asked them questions about Greenwich, Cutty Sark and the Maritime Museum.

• • •

"Interesting person," said Olivia after they left the woman.

"Yes, it was a nice chat," said Jay.

They walked until they could see Tower Bridge and the Tower of London in the distance.

5   "The Museum of London's near there," said Holly. "I'm sorry we never found the answer to that question from the challenge. You know, the oldest thing in the City of London."

"Did your grandma tell you the answer?" asked Gwen.

"I haven't seen her since the challenge," said Dave. "And I can't send 10 her a message. No mobile, remember?"

"Now I *really* want to know the answer," said Gwen.

"I don't care about that," said Jay. "I'm just enjoying this walk by the river. The Thames looks great in the sun, and look, there's even a little beach by this part of the river."

15   "*That's* the answer!" said Gwen. "The oldest thing in the City of London is the river. It was here before there was anything else, right?"

"Hey, I think you're right." said Dave. "Wait a moment. I've still got that letter." He took it out of his jacket pocket. "Look at the second part," he said, and showed his friends the letter. "'Your answer must *arrive* in one hour'. *Arrive* is in capital letters. The letters in 'arrive' spell 'a river'!"

"Oh, it was an easy one!" said Olivia. "We just didn't see it!" 5

"Are we *sure* that's the right answer?" asked Holly.

"Well, I can't phone Granny Rose to find out," said Dave.

"Yes, you can!" said Holly. "Look, there's one of those new public phone and wi-fi points over there."

Dave went to phone his grandmother. 10

"Her number is easy to remember," he said over his shoulder. "It's all twos, fours and eights."

A few minutes later he came back. "Yes, that's the right answer," he shouted. "She said I'm very clever, and I've agreed to meet her in that Casa Coffee place again next Sunday." 15

"*You're* very clever?" said Gwen. "*I* found the answer! I'm going to come with you on Sunday – to make sure she knows it was me!"

"Let's all go," said Olivia. "We can thank your grandmother for the fun challenge."

• • •

"I'm surprised to see *all* of you here," said Granny Rose to the six 20 friends. It was the next Sunday, and they were all in Casa Coffee. "I only expected Dave." She was with her Silver Surfer friends round a big table. They all had laptops and tablets again. "We're finding out how to make websites," she said. "We want to have a website for our club, but we have no idea how to make one." 25

"Oh, I know how to do that," said Dave. "But listen, it was Gwen who found the answer to your last question, not me."

The other Silver Surfers looked up from their screens and smiled.

"Well done, Gwen!" said Granny Rose.

"And they all joined me in the tech-free week," said Dave. "It was fun! 30 We communicated in other ways, and we've had a great time together."

"I see," said Granny Rose. "And have you used your phone or the internet in the last seven days?"

"No, I haven't," said Dave. "Not even for one minute. None of us has."

"Well, I'm very impressed!" said Granny Rose. She thought for a moment. "So you know how to make websites, Dave?" she said.

"Yeah, it's easy," said Dave. "I've done a couple of sites for clubs at school."

5   "How about this? You teach us how, to make a website with simple step-by-step instructions, and I get you that game you wanted after all."

"Game?"

"What was it? *Wizards on Skates*?"

"Oh, *Skateboarding Wizards II*," said Dave. He thought for a moment.
10 "It's weird. A week ago, I really wanted that game, and now I don't. Not really."

"Anyway, that game was new *last* week," said Luke. "There are different new games *this* week."

"I've got a better idea," said Dave. "I'll help you with your site, and
15 you buy lemonade and some of the cakes here for my friends and me. This place is paradise if you love cakes."

"OK, that's very nice of you, Dave. And it's the right thing to do. Friendship is much more important than computer games! Six lemonades and cakes coming right up!"

7 Epilogue

It was one month later. The friends were sitting in Casa Coffee again, but Dave was not with them. He was at another table and was talking happily to the Silver Surfers.

"Dave's really helping them a lot, isn't he?" said Holly.

"Yeah, but it only took them a few hours to make their website. With 5 his help they got better and better at it. They finished it a couple of weeks ago," said Gwen. "What's he doing now?"

"Maybe he's fixing their computers," said Olivia.

"No, I don't think so," said Luke. "I think they were already able to do that without his help." 10

At that moment, Dave came over to their table.

"Are we allowed to know what you're doing with the Silver Surfers now?" asked Luke. "Can we convince you to tell us or is it some big secret?"

"No secret," said Dave. "We put some more of those clues for Tube 15 stations in emojis on the site. People love it! The Silver Surfers can't believe their eyes! Now we're getting hundreds of visitors every day. People from countries all over the world are solving our Tube station emoji puzzles, and they're sending us new ones too."

"Can we see?" asked Holly. 20

"Sure you can take a look at it!" said Dave. "You can borrow my tablet."

He went to get it from the other table, then came back and gave it to Holly.

"You weren't joking, were you?" she said, and showed the tablet to the others. "Look at all of those emoji Tube station puzzles!" 25

"Hundreds of people in many different countries have commented," said Dave.

"How many?" Luke asked.

"*Hundreds!*" repeated Dave.

"I'm impressed!" said Luke. "But you can't do it forever, can you? 30 There aren't enough Tube stations."

"I've started a new website with a new type of puzzle," said Dave. "It's the titles of films, TV shows and books – in emojis!"

Dave took his tablet back from Holly and tapped the screen. Now it showed a new website. There was a picture of Dave's face, and the title was *Dave's Emoji Puzzles*.

"Now you're just showing off, aren't you?" said Luke.

5   "Well, yes," said Dave. "But showing off is *lots* of fun, isn't it?"

"So how's your new website going?" asked Holly. "You've wasted your time if nobody visits it, haven't you?"

"It's only been online for a few days, but the Silver Surfers' site links to it, so I've had hundreds of visitors already. I think it's going to be *big!*

Exercises

1 What happened at Casa Coffee? (Part 1)

a) *Are the sentences below right or wrong?*

	right	wrong
1. Dave got to the café after his friends.	✓	
2. Luke and Jay enjoyed their cakes.	✓	
3. There was still cake for Jay and Luke's friends.		✗
4. Olivia, Holly, Gwen and Dave bought more cake.		✗
5. They ordered *(bestellten)* one drink each.		✗

b) *Correct the sentences that are wrong.*

c) *Answer the questions.*

1. Why don't Dave's parents give him computer games?
2. What do Dave and his friends say about older people and technology?
3. What does Granny Rose say when she hears this?
4. Why does the Silver Surfer club have this name?

2 All about communication (Part 1)

a) *How often do you do these things? Number them 1 to 5.*
(1 is the most often.)

5 Check your e-mail
2 Send a message from your phone
1 Find out information from a website
4 Call somebody on the phone
3 Take a photo with your phone

b) *Do you use different forms of communication with your family than you do with your friends? Why/why not?*

3 The adventure begins (Part 2)

Pick (wähle … aus) *the best answer.*

1. What does Dave receive from the Silver Surfers?
   a) An invitation to a party
   b) An invitation to solve some puzzles
   c) A challenge to spend a week without any internet

2. If Dave can't do the tasks and puzzles, then for a week he can't …
   a) play computer games or use the internet.
   b) play computer games or use the internet or his smartphone.
   c) use the internet, but he can still use his smartphone.

3. Who is going to help Dave and Luke?
   a) Holly, Olivia and Jay
   b) Only Olivia
   c) Holly and Olivia

4 At the National Maritime Museum (Part 3)

a) *Put the events in the correct order. Number them 1 to 6.*

   3 A Dave looks up some information on the internet.
   1 B Dave meets Luke, Holly and Olivia in Greenwich Park.
   2 C Dave receives a new challenge from the Silver Surfers.
   4 D The friends go to the National Maritime Museum.
   5 E The kids send a picture of the answer to the first riddle.
   6 F Dave receives a riddle from the Silver Surfers.

b) *Answer the questions.*

   1. What kind of a ship do the friends hope to find in the National Maritime Museum?
   2. Why aren't any of the ships in the National Maritime Museum the answer to the riddle?

5 Your turn … (Part 3)

a) *You are the man who took the photo of the friends.*
   Write a message to the other Silver Surfers. Explain what happened.

b) *Can you guess what Dave and his friends must do for the next challenge? Talk to a partner about it.*

6 Journey on the Tube (Part 4)

Match each station with what happened there (one or two events).

1. near Cutty Sark

2. Elephant and Castle

3. Euston

4. London Bridge

5. Waterloo

a) Holly solves the whole puzzle.
b) Dave looks up the meaning of an emoji online.
c) Holly says they must go back to London Bridge.
d) They receive the first part of the puzzle.
e) Luke and Holly fight about *(streiten sich über)* the best way to get to Elephant and Castle.
f) Dave sends the first selfie to the Silver Surfers.
g) Dave finds an envelope with the next challenge.
h) Holly solves an emoji puzzle with just the first emoji.

7 Stations and emojis (Part 4)

a) *Follow the friends' journey on a London Tube map. To find a map, go to the 'Transport for London' website.*

b) *Describe another journey. Your partner must follow it on the map. Does he/she end up where you want him/her to go?*

c) *Here are the names of more London Tube stations. Choose at least three and draw emojis for them. Then ask other students to guess the stations.*

Angel	Bank	Blackhorse Road
Green Park	King's Cross	Old Street
Queen's Park	Redbridge	Seven Sisters
Tower Hill	White City	Wood Green

8 What on earth happened?! (Part 5)

a) *These are parts of a letter that Dave writes to his cousin about the challenge. Read the first part and find the correct words from the box below.*

> notice | best | leaving | quickly | exactly | of course |
> two of them | oldest | checked | forum | embarrassed | clever

… We had to find the **(1)** thing in the City of London in **(2)** one hour! So we thought that the Museum of London was the **(3)** place to go. First, we **(4)** the internet to find out how to get there. From an answer on a **(5)** I found that we needed to take bus 59. It was just **(6)**, so we jumped on **(7)**. What I didn't **(8)** was that the answer wasn't right. **(9)**, Holly and Olivia found out first. They **(10)** think that they're so **(11)**! We were going in the wrong direction and I was so **(12)**! …

b) *Read the second part and find the correct words from the box.*

> panicked | app | discussion | take part in | texted | finally |
> whole | upset | downloaded

… Then I **(1)** a good transport **(2)** and we got on the right bus! When we got to the museum there were only 15 minutes left! We went to the prehistoric section, where we had a big **(3)** about the answer and I **(4)**. **(5)**, with only two minutes left, I **(6)** the Silver Surfers our best guess: the things in the prehistoric section. And it was wrong! Now I have to live for a **(7)** week without my smartphone, or the internet or my computer games!! I'm so **(8)**! Why did I **(9)** this silly challenge?
Let's talk soon! I can text you when I can use my phone again!
Yours,
Dave

9 Communicating face-to-face (Part 6)

a) *Match the events with the reasons for them.*

1. There are not many people in the park
2. Jay made a mistake about the weather
3. Dave isn't going to use the internet
4. Dave thinks the week is going to be awful
5. All the friends decide not to use the internet for a week
6. Jay can't send messages to his other friends

a) because he looked up the forecast for a different London.
b) because he wants to follow the rules of the game.
c) because he won't get messages from his friends.
d) because the week with no internet has already started.
e) because it isn't the weekend.
f) because they don't want Dave to feel alone.

b) *Which of these experiences did the friends have during their week?*

1. They spent more time together.
2. They found that it's easier to organise places to meet.
3. The challenge was difficult for their friendship.
4. They talked to an interesting person.
5. They learned about some London history.
6. The week was very difficult and they were happy that it was over.

10 Fun with websites (Part 7)

a) *What is Dave doing with the Silver Surfers?*

b) *Why has Dave started a new project, and what is it?*

c) *Can you solve the puzzle from Dave's website on page 36?*

d) *You want to start a new website for young people. What is it going to be about? How is it going to be similar to or different from other websites? Discuss your ideas in groups.*

Vocabulary

pl. plural
to **rain** Vokabeln aus Green Line 2, Unit 5 und/oder Green Line 2 Baden-Württemberg, Unit 4
wi-fi neue Vokabeln, die bis Green Line 2, Unit 5 bzw. Green Line 2 Baden-Württemberg, Unit 4 nicht vorkommen

Before you read
Page 4
wi-fi ['waɪfaɪ] WLAN
oyster ['ɔɪstə] Auster

Part 1
Page 5
pile [paɪl] Stapel
to **pick up** [ˌpɪk ˈʌp] *hier:* nehmen
to **type** [taɪp] tippen
I'll … [aɪl] Ich werde …
to **rain** [reɪn] regnen
mine [maɪn] mein
to **fix** [fɪks] reparieren
washing machine ['wɒʃɪŋ məˌʃiːn] Waschmaschine
pipe [paɪp] Rohr, Rohrleitung
to **tap** [tæp] (an)tippen
app [æp] App
instant message [ˌɪnstənt 'mesɪdʒ] Sofortnachricht
practical ['præktɪkl] praktisch
mobile ['məʊbaɪl] Handy; Mobiltelefon

Page 6
to **arrive** [ə'raɪv] ankommen
plate [pleɪt] Teller
empty ['emti] leer
for yourselves [fə jɔː'selvz] für euch

Page 7
to **borrow** ['bɒrəʊ] ausleihen
delicious [de'lɪʃəs] lecker
to **pretend** [prɪ'tend] so tun als ob
to **share** [ʃeə] teilen
to **overreact** [ˌəʊvəri'ækt] überreagieren
to **push** [pʊʃ] schubsen
to **go on sth** ['gəʊ ɒn] *hier:* verschüttet werden
to **calm down** [ˌkɑːm 'daʊn] sich beruhigen
the two of them [ðə 'tuː ˌəv ðəm] beide
to **mediate** ['miːdieɪt] vermitteln
fight [faɪt] Kampf; Streit
to **turn to** ['tɜːn tə] sich zuweden
what to do [ˌwɒt tə'duː] *hier:* was wir tun können
waitress ['weɪtrɪs] Kellnerin
to **joke** [dʒəʊk] scherzen
wizard ['wɪzəd] Zauberer
to **have to** ['hæv tə] müssen

Page 8
to **spend** [spend] verbringen
to **waste** [weɪst] verschwenden
understanding [ˌʌndə'stændɪŋ] Verständnis
teen [tiːn] Jugendliche/-r
media ['miːdiə] Medien
newspaper ['njuːsˌpeɪpə] Zeitung
tablet ['tæblət] Tablet
to **e-mail** ['iːmeɪl] mailen
letter ['letə] *hier:* Brief
print [prɪnt] gedruckt, Druck-
copy ['kɒpi] Exemplar
cannot ['kænɒt] kann nicht
kid [kɪd] Jugendliche/-r; Kind

Page 9
grandmother ['grænˌmʌðə] Großmutter
to **point to** ['pɔɪnt tə] zeigen auf
laptop ['læptɒp] Laptop
for [fɔː] *hier:* wegen
hair [heə] Haare

mad [mæd] verrückt
interest ['ɪntrəst] Interesse
communication [kəˌmjuːnɪˈkeɪʃn]
    Kommunikation
to stay in touch (with) [ˌsteɪ ɪn ˈtʌtʃ wɪð]
    in Kontakt bleiben (mit)
opinion [əˈpɪnjən] Meinung
clever [ˈklevə] schlau; klug
she will [ˌʃiː ˈwɪl] sie wird
She may, she may not. [meɪ] Vielleicht (wird
    sie es tun), vielleicht auch nicht
mysterious [mɪˈstɪəriəs] geheimnisvoll

Part 2
Page 10
headphones (pl.) [ˈhedfəʊnz] Kopfhörer
to make sb do sth [ˌmeɪk ˈduː] jmdn. dazu
    bringen, etw. zu tun
to cry [kraɪ] hier: schreien; rufen
with a very big head [wɪðˌə ˌveri bɪg ˈhed]
    und ein Angeber
whenever [wenˈevə] jedes Mal, wenn
more than I do [ˌmɔː ðænˌˈiː ˌduː]
    mehr als ich
to show off [ʃəʊˌˈɒf] angeben
front door [ˌfrʌntˈdɔː] Haustür
click [klɪk] Klicken, Klick
knob [nɒb] Griff

Page 11
to cook [kʊk] kochen
to be on [biˌˈɒn] hier: laufen
mess [mes] Unordnung; Durcheinander
jacket [ˈdʒækɪt] Jacke
to carry [ˈkæri] tragen
upstairs [ʌpˈsteəz] hier: nach oben;
    ins Obergeschoss
to turn on [ˌtɜːnˌˈɒn] etw. einschalten
downstairs [daʊnˈsteəz] hier: unten;
    im Untergeschoss
video [ˈvɪdiəʊ] Video
screen [skriːn] Bildschirm
If you can't do this [ɪf juː ˈkɑːnt duː ˌðis]
    Wenn du das nicht (tun) kannst
to come onto [kʌmˌˈɒntuː] erscheinen auf
to agree [əˈgriː] hier: einwilligen

Page 12
since [sɪns] seit
to take part in [ˌteɪk ˈpɑːt (ɪn)]
    teilnehmen an
camping [ˈkæmpɪŋ] Camping; Zelten
to miss sth [mɪs] etw. versäumen
to text [tekst] eine SMS schicken
pocket [ˈpɒkɪt] (Hosen)tasche
discussion [dɪˈskʌʃn] Diskussion

Part 3
Page 13
wind [wɪnd] Wind
to reach [riːtʃ] erreichen
bench [benʃ] Sitzbank

Page 14
riddle [ˈrɪdl] Rätsel
I don't get it. [ˌaɪ dəʊnt ˈget ɪt]
    Das verstehe ich nicht.
plus [plʌs] plus
as soon as [əz ˈsuːnˌəz] sobald
indoors [ɪnˈdɔːz] drinnen
to search for sth [ˈsɜːtʃ fɔː] (nach)
    etw. suchen
Hurry up! [ˈhʌriˌʌp] Beeil dich!
to take time [ˌteɪk ˈtaɪm] hier: zu lange
    brauchen
nearly [ˈnɪəli] fast
National Maritime Museum
    [ˌnæʃnl ˈmærɪtaɪm mjuːˈziːəm]
    Nationales Schifffahrtsmuseum
entrance [ˈentrəns] Eingang

Page 15
to worry [ˈwʌri] sich Sorgen machen
still [stɪl] dennoch, trotzdem
to blow away [ˌbləʊˌəˈweɪ] wegwehen
to go crazy [gəʊ ˈkreɪzi] verrückt werden
to slow down [sləʊ ˈdaʊn] hier: langsamer
    laufen
faster [ˈfɑːstə] schneller
work of art [wɜːkˌəvˈɑːt] Kunstwerk
term [tɜːm] Semester
battle [ˈbætl] Schlacht
eighteen something [eɪˈtiːn ˌsʌmθɪŋ]
    achtzehnhundert irgendwas

onto [ˈɒntu:] auf
right now [ˌraɪt ˈnaʊ] *hier:* gerade
disaster [dɪˈzɑːstə] Katastrophe
section [ˈsekʃən] Abteilung

Page 28
prehistoric [ˌpriːhɪˈstɒrɪk] prähistorisch
There's no such thing as . . .
   [ðeəs ˈnəʊ sʌtʃ ˌθɪŋ ˌæz] Es gibt keine …
agony aunt [ˈægəniˌɑːnt]
   Kummerkastentante
watch [wɒtʃ] Uhr
to cry [kraɪ] *hier:* weinen

Part 6
Page 29
flower [ˈflaʊə] Blume
beautiful [ˈbjuːtɪfəl] schön
weekday [ˈwiːkdeɪ] Wochentag
weather forecast [ˈweðə ˌfɔːkɑːst]
   Wettervorhersage
thunder [ˈθʌndə] Donner
lightning [ˈlaɪtnɪŋ] Blitz
Never mind the weather!
   [ˌnevə maɪnd ðə ˈweðə] Das Wetter ist
   doch egal!
to do about [ˈduː ˌəˌbaʊt] unternehmen
   wegen
compromise [ˈkɒmprəmaɪz] Kompromiss
promise [ˈprɒmɪs] Versprechen
to make a bet [ˈmeɪk ə ˌbet] wetten
to feel left out [ˌfiːl left ˈaʊt]
   sich ausgeschlossen fühlen
to stay away from [ˌsteɪ əˈweɪ frəm]
   fernbleiben von; meiden
for fun [fə ˈfʌn] zum Spaß
to act like [ˈækt laɪk] so tun als ob
what on earth [ˌwɒt ˌɒn ˈɜːθ]
   was um alles in der Welt
wouldn't be [ˈwʊdənt biː] wäre nicht
power cut [ˈpaʊə ˌkʌt] Stromausfall
to go black [ˌgəʊ ˈblæk] schwarz werden
candlelight [ˈkændlaɪt] Kerzenlicht

Page 30
nasty [ˈnɑːsti] garstig; gemein
social network [ˌsəʊʃl ˈnetwɜːk] soziales
   Netzwerk
attention [əˈtenʃn] Aufmerksamkeit
cyber bully [ˌsaɪbə ˈbʊli] *jemand, der
   andere in sozialen Netzwerken belästigt
   oder mobbt*
to block [blɒk] blockieren
to agree [əˈgriː] zustimmen
I'm in. [aɪmˈɪn] Ich bin dabei.
to post [pəʊst] online stellen
offline [ˈɒflaɪn] offline
There's no need to be . . . .
   [ðeəz ˌnəʊ ˈniːd tə biː]
   Du brauchst nicht …zu sein.
upset [ʌpˈset] aufgebracht; bestürzt
forever [fəˈrevə] für immer; ewig
technology-free [tekˈnɒlədʒi friː]
   technologiefrei
landline [ˈlændlaɪn] Festnetz
myself [maɪˈself] selbst; selber
I'm enjoying myself [aɪm ɪnˈdʒɔɪŋ maɪˌself]
   Es macht mir Spaß
face-to-face [ˌfeɪstəˈfeɪs] persönlich;
   von Angesicht zu Angesicht

Page 31
walk [wɔːk] Spaziergang
all the way [al ðə ˈweɪ] den ganzen Weg
here we come [hɪə wi: ˈkʌm] wir kommen
Canary Wharf [kəˈneəri ˌwɔːf] *Bürogebäude-
   komplex in den Londoner Docklands*
dock [dɒk] Dock; Hafenanlage
to get out of [get ˌaʊt ˌəv]
   herauskommen aus
office block [ˈɒfɪs ˌblɒk] Bürogebäude
to change [tʃeɪndʒ] (sich) ändern
bang [bæŋ] peng
Victorian [vɪkˈtɔːriːən] viktorianisch
title [ˈtaɪtl] *hier:* Buchtitel
Spain [speɪn] Spanien

Page 32
to care (about) [ˈkeərˌəˌbaʊt] wichtig
   nehmen; sich interessieren (für)
beach [biːtʃ] Strand

to **phone** [fəʊn] anrufen
wi-fi point [ˈwaɪfaɪ ˌpɔɪnt] Hotspot
(öffentlicher drahtloser Internet-
zugriffspunkt)
to **expect sb** [ɪkˈspekt] jmdn. erwarten
round [raʊnd] um herum
tech-free [ˈtek friː] technologiefrei
in other ways [ɪn ˈʌðə weɪz]
   auf andere Weise
none [nʌn] keine(r, s)

to **be impressed** [bi ɪmˈprest]
   beeindruckt sein
site [saɪt] Website
step-by-step [ˌstepbaɪˈstep]
   Schritt-für-Schritt-
weird [wɪəd] merkwürdig; seltsam
paradise [ˈpærədaɪs] Paradies
friendship [ˈfrendʃɪp] Freundschaft
coming right up [ˈkʌmɪŋ raɪt ˌʌp]
   kommt/kommen sofort

Part 7
to **be allowed to** (do sth) [biː əˈlaud tə]
   (etw. tun) dürfen
to **solve** [sɒlv] lösen
to **repeat** [rɪˈpiːt] wiederholen

How is … going? [haʊ ɪz … ˈgəʊɪŋ]
   Wie läuft's mit …
I think it's going to be big!
   [i: ˌθɪŋk ɪts gəʊɪŋ tə biː ˈbɪg] Ich glaube,
   sie (die Website) wird ein großer Erfolg.

Exercises
to **order** [ˈɔːdə] bestellen

to **pick** [pɪk] auswählen

to **fight** (about) [faɪt əˈbaʊt]
   sich streiten über

Solutions

Before you read the story

1   Your digital life
individuelle Schülerlösungen

2   What do you know about London?
1. a,   2. c,   3. a,   4. b,   5. c,   6. a,   7. b,   8. a

Exercises

1   What happened at Casa Coffee? (Part 1)
a) 1. right,   2. right,   3 wrong,   4. wrong,   5. wrong
b) 3. There was no cake left.   4. Olivia, Holly, Gwen and Dave didn't have enough money to buy cake.   5. They ordered three glasses of lemonade and an extra glass.
c) 1. They say he spends too much time on his computer.   2. They have no idea about technology.   3. Many of them <u>do</u> understand technology.   4. They surf the internet and they all have silver hair.

2   All about communication (Part 1)
a) + b) *individuelle Schülerlösungen*

3   The adventure begins (Part 2)
1. b,   2. b,   3. c

4   At the National Maritime Museum (Part 3)
a) 1. B,   2. F,   3. A,   4. D,   5. E,   6. c
b) 1. They hope to find a ship with sails that is indoors so that no wind can reach it.
   2. The wind <u>can</u> reach the ships, through the open windows.

5   Your turn … (Part 3)
a) Model answer: Dave and his friends came out of the museum and found *Nelson's Ship in a Bottle*. They asked me to take a photo of them in front of it. I took the photo, and then I left the envelope with the next challenge and the day tickets on a bench. I saw Dave pick it up.
b) *individuelle Schülerlösungen*

6 Journey on the Tube (Part 4)
1. d, e; 2. f, b; 3. c; 4. h; 5. a, g

7 Stations and emojis (Part 4)
a)–c) *individuelle Schülerlösungen*

8 What on earth happened?! (Part 5)
a) 1. oldest, 2. exactly, 3. best, 4. checked, 5. forum, 6. leaving,
   7. quickly, 8. notice, 9. of course, 10. two of them, 11. clever,
   12. embarrassed
b) 1. downloaded, 2. app, 3. discussion, 4. panicked, 5. finally,
   6. texted, 7. whole, 8. upset, 9. take part in

9 Communicating face-to-face (Part 6)
a) 1. e, 2. a, 3. b, 4. c, 5. f, 6. d
b) 1, 4, 5

10 Fun with websites (Part 7)
a) *They put more Tube station emoji puzzles on the Silver Surfers' website.*
b) *Dave has started a new website with a new type of puzzle. It's the titles of films, TV shows and books in emojis.*
c) *Harry Potter and the Half-Blood Prince/Harry Potter und der Halbblutprinz*
d) *individuelle Schülerlösungen*